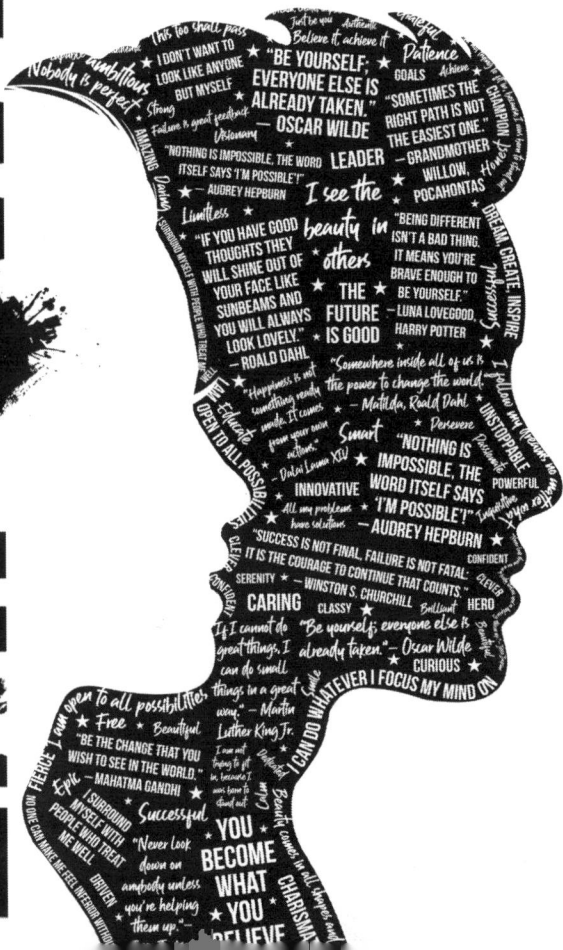

First published in Great Britain in 2025 by:

YoungWriters®
Est. 1991

Young Writers
Remus House
Coltsfoot Drive
Peterborough
PE2 9BF
Telephone: 01733 890066
Website: www.youngwriters.co.uk

⭐ FOREWORD ⭐

Since 1991, here at Young Writers we have celebrated the awesome power of creative writing, especially in young adults where it can serve as a vital method of expressing their emotions and views about the world around them. In every poem we see the effort and thought that each student published in this book has put into their work and by creating this anthology we hope to encourage them further with the ultimate goal of sparking a life-long love of writing.

Our latest competition for secondary school students, Empowered, challenged young writers to consider what was important to them. We wanted to give them a voice, the chance to express themselves freely and honestly, something which is so important for these young adults to feel confident and listened to. They could give an opinion, share a memory, consider a dilemma, impart advice or simply write about something they love. There were no restrictions on style or subject so you will find an anthology brimming with a variety of poetic styles and topics. We hope you find it as absorbing as we have.

We encourage young writers to express themselves and address subjects that matter to them, which sometimes means writing about sensitive or contentious topics. If you have been affected by any issues raised in this book, details on where to find help can be found at **www.youngwriters.co.uk/support**

✭ CONTENTS ✭

Evie Birkbeck (12)	60	Ashton-Lewis Kennedy (13)	103
Olivia Allott (13)	61	Joey Garner (12)	104
Finley Newton (12)	62	Halli Beckett (11)	105
Leila Stephens (13)	63	Seth Rouane (12)	106
Will Kelly (11)	64	Jack Hirst (12)	107
Hasan Bilyal (11)	65	Charlie Johnson (12)	108
Jessica Hampshire (13)	66	Olivia Horner (13)	109
George Saunders (13)	67	Jack Garrett (13)	110
Jax Adkins (13)	68	Harley Hale (12)	111
Franceska Woolley (13)	69	Nevin Roby (12)	112
Ellie Line (13)	70	Evie Harris (12)	113
Rose Bradley (11)	71	Jake Beardsley (13)	114
Ross Mitchell (12)	72	Freya Atkin (12)	115
Jamie Lawless (12)	73	Mineda Milasauske (13)	116
Ted Morgan (13)	74	Pippa Mitchell (12) & Scarlett	117
Millie Hamshaw (13)	75	Kaylum Donnelly-Dodd (12)	118
Summer North (12)	76	Charlotte Wilcock (12)	119
Nicola Tomasiewicz (13)	77	Alfie Stark (12)	120
Hollie Backhouse (13)	78	Bradley Horner (13) & Jake	121
Danny Allwood (12)	79	Harrison Yarrow (11)	122
Mia Glossop (13)	80	Charley-Jo Rickson (13)	123
Lily Beardsley (12)	81	Connor Swift (11)	124
Scarlett Cantrell (13)	82	Gracie-Mai White (12)	125
Charlie Addy (12)	83	Niamh Higham (11)	126
Rose Outram (13)	84	Matthew Harrop (12)	127
Cameron Willis (12)	85	Grayson Abbott (12)	128
Millie Fenton-Wightman (11)	86	Orla Gannon (11)	129
Matty Beckitt (12)	87	Dionne Kesse-Oware (11)	130
Lois Cooke (13)	88	Olivia Birch (12)	131
Isacc Thorpe (11)	89	Summer Whitehead (12)	132
Chloe Hatfield (13)	90	Darcie Watkins (12)	133
Bodhi Connolly (12)	91	Tommy Dudley (13)	134
Emily Hampshire (12)	92	Annabelle Young (13)	135
Noah Bennett (12)	93	Tayla Shaw (12)	136
Eva Whike-Blunt (12)	94	Logan Bennett (12)	137
Toby Phillips (12)	95		
Ayla Nuttall (12)	96		
Thomas Meggitt (13)	97		

Tettenhall College, Tettenhall

Mena Claiyapartho (12)	98	Frankie Wilkins (12)	138
Harriett Clarke (12)	99	Zara Purchase (12)	140
Lewis Hawley (12)	100	Lily Stonehouse (12)	141
Ruby Grocott (13)	101	Honey Smith (12)	142
Lorelai Jones-Lee (13)	102	Mia Kearns (12)	143
		Arjun Kahlon (12)	144

Elia Jackson (12)	145
Harvey Westwood-Hilbert (12)	146
Nevaeh Jackson (12)	147
Dhea Mair (12)	148
Abigail Davis (12)	149
Jair Benjamin (12)	150
Taisiia Kazakevych (12)	151
Amelia Donoghue (15)	152
Pennie-May Shaw (16)	153
Finlay Baldock (12)	154

The Bishop's Stortford High School, Bishop's Stortford

Ruan Kellard (15)	155
Isaac Jones (15)	156
Nadim Shawky (15)	158
Thomas Cleggett (12)	159
Luke Thorogood (11)	160
Anthony Long (11)	161
Ethan Moran (12)	162
Ralf Smith (12)	163
Codey Taylor-Francis (11)	164
Felix Watson (11)	165
Freddie Smith (12)	166
Finley Morris (12)	167
Xander Spicer (12)	168
Jack Wren (11)	169
Dylan McCabe (12)	170
Kieran Dedman (12)	171
Oscar Collins (12)	172
Efe Kakacoglu (12)	173
Frederick Jobber (13)	174
Otto Kormis (12)	175

Thornaby Academy, Thornaby

Amy Sutherland (12)	176
Beaux Waterhouse (12)	178
Willow Cooper Wilkinson (11)	179
Michelle Fegbada (13)	180
Lillie Manning (15)	181
Ralphy Dollard (12)	182
Mirab Shahzad (14)	183

Harley Alyssa-May Atkins (12)	184
Autumn Day (13)	185
Sophie Iveson (11)	186
Reece Taylor (14)	187
Kacey-May Lenighan (12)	188
Kejsi Diva (12)	189
Rutaab Asim (13)	190
Patience Micah (14)	191
Felicity Robson (12)	192
Scarlett Foster (12)	193
Amelia Galloway (11)	194
Tyler Hobbs (12)	195
Sienna Trotter (11)	196
Sophie Wendy Bown (12)	197
Sreya Sujith Nair (14)	198
Nellie Henry (12)	199

Venture Academy, Henley-In-Arden

Cian Dooley (11)	200
Chloe Roebuck (16)	201
Quinn Vickery (13)	202
George Derry (12)	203
Josh Edwards (16)	204
Jake Hill (15)	205

The Poems

Misuse Of Power

Fires rage,
Blood is spilt,
The world is at war for the third time in a row.

Nature withers and dies,
Buildings are reduced to mere ashes,
It's not fair.

Families separated.
Children in floods of tears.
Guilty parents having to say the one thing they shouldn't,
"I'm sorry, the war is getting worse."

Students perched diligently at desks in the countryside.
Eyes glazed,
Pale faces like the fallen dead,
Worrying endlessly,
What will happen to our families?

I never knew greed was this powerful, that it could tear our
world apart.
And I,
You may wonder,
Where do I come in all of this mess?
I just sit and wonder why.
Why did they do this to my home...?

Siyana Fazal (11)
Hallfield School, Edgbaston

The Planet

The world we live in is full of life and mystery,
From sunny days to starry nights.
The sturdy forests stand tall,
The humongous oceans across the globe.

But slowly, change is on its way,
The rivers used to be so clean,
The air was fresh, the grass was bright green.
But now trees are being cut,
And plastic piles up all around the world.

The sun can warm you up, but can also burn you,
The weather is changing, so we must learn to use less
plastic and waste less,
And plant more trees to know our planet.

It's not too late to save the environment,
So by working together, hand in hand
We can save the beauty of the world.

Jai Malhi (12)
Hallfield School, Edgbaston

Time

Time doesn't shout, time doesn't wait
Time slips through cracks, time opens gates
A quiet whisper, soft and slow
Then suddenly, it's time to go

One moment here, the next one passed
You blink and things have changed so fast
The tree we climbed when we were small
Now sees less, big and tall

It's in the laughs, the fears, the tries
In morning sun and evening skies
You cannot pause it, can't rewind
But time leaves memories behind

So live each hour like it's gold
Be brave, be strong, be gold, bold
Time movies with grace
And never stays in place.

Edward Bryan (12)
Hallfield School, Edgbaston

All Collected

Sports cars, race cars, SUVs,
Prowling concrete roads, chasing time,
Choose what you do,
Own your path
Earn your stay,
Every road a start,
Every turn a chance.

Give yourself to the power
To do what you want,
To outrun the ordinary,
To chase what you desire.
All collected
In the car you choose.

Konstantin von Wedel (12)
Hallfield School, Edgbaston

Poison Burn

Our climate is getting hotter,
It might sound nice, but you are wrong,
Get your head out of the gutter,
Because the birds will sing their song.

There are things we all should do,
To make it cleaner for me and you,
Nothing alive can evolve in time,
So we will have to solve this crime.

If you deny it when it's true,
Then what the hell is wrong with you?
There is evidence you can't deny,
And I know you feel it, too.

Between us two, there's something we need to do,
Help others, plants, animals and yourself,
Otherwise, you'll lose yourself,
Help feel better with yourself,
But it also helps the world as well.

We are the poison of this world,
And if we keep going, we'll get burned.

Micah Donaldson (14)
James Calvert Spence College, Amble

The Broken Clock

Years of protest
Years of rebellion
And years of change
Just to go back in time
And undo it all

The acceptance
The equality
The freedom
And the change
Everything the former generations fought for
Becoming this generation's battle

They fill our heads with their false words
Their white lies
Telling us what we want to hear
But then do the opposite

They claim it's for our own good
But what will they do
When the battle restarts
Where the people don't obediently stand by them
When the suicide rate rises?

Times are changing
But not for the better
Times are changing
And the broken clock
Is in reverse.

Maisie Crone (14)
James Calvert Spence College, Amble

Equality Is Everything

The world needs to change,
Women are still being restrained,
Used like an item,
When will we learn?
We need to change this cruel, cruel world,
No hands should be thrown,
Just leave them alone,
They don't need to cook,
They don't need to clean,
Marriage is a partnership with trust, a team,
When will people wake up from their dreams,
And realise this still goes on,
Although it is wrong?
This mental, verbal, physical abuse,
It's not something to be reclused,
So when will people wake up and see
The world is not how it is meant to be,
It should be full of equality.

Chloe Conway (14)
James Calvert Spence College, Amble

Unheard Voices, Equal Volume

A truth covered,
Beneath a lie told,
In a crowded room,
No real stories told.

Why raise your voice if the pain is distant?
If your privilege is a shield?
Why risk breaking it?
At the end of the day,
It's the poor who pay,
While the rich parade.

So, how long will this charade go on for?
How many will go without a voice?
If it's equality, then why don't they listen
When we are all speaking with the same volume?

Break the chains society holds,
Give hope to others,
Because
Hope is the only thing stronger than fear.

Anya Wright (13)
James Calvert Spence College, Amble

Burn It Down

Be a good soldier
Don't let the pressure get to your shoulders
The voices bring you up and down
With the fire inside, just let it burn it down
If the people don't see you
Make them hear you
If it's on TV or the stereo
Don't make yourself mysterio
Light the world up with your presence
Make the world feel your essence
Change this society before you become a dead man
Anyone can do it; child, man, or woman
Flipping the scales can take a word or phrase
Because this fire burns
Always.

Riley Baker (14)
James Calvert Spence College, Amble

Superpower

If you had a superpower, what would you do?
Would you fly away or paint the world black and blue?
Would you save the world with your tremendous might?
Or sit down and watch the world fight?
Would you be the world's brightest star?
Or burn out faster than any car?
Why should you change because you have powers?
Be yourself, sing your favourite song in the shower.
Be you,
Don't be blue.
You don't get how many people need you.

Jackson Purvis (14)

James Calvert Spence College, Amble

Mannequin

Still I stand, dressed in directed expectations
On my own little stage, ignored
Like a show without a front page

Still I stand, waiting to walk to no avail
Placed on a floor I have no control over
Like a trapped bird held down in a cage

Still I stand, tired as I fall apart
Crying for help from my covered mouth
Like a mannequin on the shelf.

Owen Gough (14)
James Calvert Spence College, Amble

Conflict, Wouldn't It All Just Be So Great?

What if we lived in a world with no conflict?
Imagine if we had learned from past mistakes?
What if people were not so greedy?
Wouldn't it all just be so great?
Imagine if young people were to have a say?
Imagine if not so many lives had been lost to wars
Started over land and religion?
Wouldn't it all just be so great?

Lilia Idle (14)
James Calvert Spence College, Amble

The School

The school is a prison
Bars on the windows
Classes - like cages
Lessons - like an inquisition
You are locked as in isolation
No hope for the next day
You live in a loop
Day by day
And you can't run away
You are trapped in the cage
This is not the end
Then everything will repeat again.

Pavlo Korablin (14)
James Calvert Spence College, Amble

I Am Now Empowered

I used the strength and the power I hold
I was too weak to break, too shy, and too cold
I always wondered if I'd ever find my way
I let my fear decide my day
I let my fear blind me.

I rushed into a dream I hadn't grown
I chased every light and sky, but on my own
What I thought was weak and not enough then
Was just a seed that wasn't ready when.

I slowed my soul and took my time
Each step I took was a step, each step I took was a climb
And in the quiet, I found my sound
I found my voice that I once thought I had lost
I'm now bold and unbound.

Now I walk with boldness in my eyes
My head is held high, and I do not hide
I rise each day with calm and fire
I am empowered, through and through
There is no need for praise, for I know what is true.

What I thought was far, I embraced it
I'm no more running but moving at my own pace
I'm no longer a girl who doubts
I'm now empowered and fearless.

Tiwa Fatoye (15)
Knole Academy, Sevenoaks

Dear Tabitha

It was a very long time ago,
When I was about seven,
She was buried head to toe,
Then arose up to Heaven.

I cried when she left,
But I didn't understand
That this was death,
Still clutched within her hand.

But she was gone now,
I was told to forget her.
Forget Gran? How?
My mind turned to a blur.

Some were happy,
They said it was better.
My dear old granny;
All she'd left was a letter:

'Dear Tabitha,
I feel my time is up,
I fear I'm dying, Tabitha,
I'm running out of luck.

Dear Tabitha,
My only friend in life
Don't be scared, my Tabitha
I'm sure you'll be all right.

Dearest Tabitha,
I leave it all to you
The whole house, my Tabitha
And all my money too.

Use it wisely, Tabitha.
I know you'll use it well.
I love you dearly, Tabitha.
You love me, too, I can tell.

I'm leaving now, my Tabitha,
We have to say goodbye.
My dearest, darling Tabitha
Go off and live your life'.

Lily Tompsett (13)
Knole Academy, Sevenoaks

Save The Planet

S o, I'm here to tell you about the planet,
A planet on which we live.
V enture off into the high mountains, deep seas.
E very inch of this luscious world is changing.

T his Earth is precious, home to thousands of species.
H elp save it as it is heating up, and is soon to flood.
E very inch of this planet could get covered in water, if we don't do something.

P luto got tossed aside, will that be Earth too?
L ove your home, you sit there complaining,
A bout politicians, but you're destroying the Earth too.
N o getting an electric car, wouldn't it help? Because electricity is hurting the Earth.
E arth, sweet Earth, it was perfect.
T he question is, what can we do about it? And I'm just as clueless as anyone else...

Lexie Goodrich (12)

Knole Academy, Sevenoaks

Education's Not Fun, But The Outcome Is

The world is always moving around, no matter what.
But sometimes it can't go on, but it does.
You must treat your education how the world treats us,
Ill, sick, injured or any kind of setback you must be through,
The thought of learning might be appalling, but your
outcome will be very different.

You could be moving from country to country in the most
luxurious clothes,
Multiple houses with several cars that go incredibly fast.
If you want that,
Do this.

Wake up happily,
Face the bullets that come at you,
Get through the day.

And one more thing,
Be the best you can be.

Sonni Howell (12)
Knole Academy, Sevenoaks

Summer Days

S ummer days make fantastic memories
U nder our feet then come many peonies
M ighty waves lapping at our feet
M usic playing in the streets
E arly morning birdsong is a treat
R ain is welcome in the glorious heat.

D azzling days skip past us again
A s the days bring us back rain
Y ellow bellows across the silent sky
S o now everyone, say hello again and fly!

Always enjoy the summer days!
Have the time of one's life!
Do not lack for excitement!
Adore the summer!

Aadya Gupta (12)
Knole Academy, Sevenoaks

Return To Me

Final days, withering away,
Everyone's emotions are as dead as day,
Say to me you will be okay,
Crumbling walls isolating me away,
My precious dog, come back to me, I pray,
Grandparent happiness disappearing day by day.

Return to me, return to me, I pray,
Nan and Grandad found a new replacement to stay,
There's something I wonder every day: why did you suddenly go away?
My childhood doesn't feel right without you today,
Return to me, return to me, I pray,
Life is not fair anyways.

Lillie Pilkington (11)
Knole Academy, Sevenoaks

Climate Change

C old turns to hot.
L ives at risk.
I magine a world of water.
M ass of dry land.
A s the ice melts.
T urning the world to fire.
E ventually, nothing will exist.

C apsized iceberg.
H appiness to sadness.
A world of destruction.
N ever leaving our sight.
G oing across the world.
E ven the animals.

The only one who can save us is *you!*

Leonie Jackson (12)
Knole Academy, Sevenoaks

Hopes And Dreams

As the light shone at the top of the mountain,
I could see my dreams ahead of me.
I ran up the mountain like a bullet,
I could see my hopes shining ahead of me like the brightest star.
I smiled like I never had before,
Watching them fly by merrily like a bird.
As my hopes and dreams flew by,
I watched them gleam in the sky,
That's when I knew what I wanted to do,
As I grow older and older.

Amelia King (12)

Knole Academy, Sevenoaks

Mother's Always Right

In the depths of the night
It brings fright
Mother's always right

Walking around
Will get you aground
But not so far around
Mother's always right

Screen time
Why not make a rhyme?
Mother's always right

Education, why not get the nation
To understand?
Mother's always right.

Eleanor Lusher-Guess (12)
Knole Academy, Sevenoaks

Best Friends

B   rilliant
E   xcellent
S   tands up for rights
T   rue friendship

F   orever
R   eally fun
I   nteresting
E   xcellent
N   oble
D   oesn't upset you.

Kayla Chapell (12)

Knole Academy, Sevenoaks

Feminist Forever

F orgives but does not forget
E mpowering
M ost beautiful
I s emotional but strong
N ever gives up
I ntelligent but not cocky
S assy
T ries to the max.

Mia Wallis-Figa (13)
Knole Academy, Sevenoaks

Hello

Hello, world.

Hello, I apologise for the world we are creating for 2100.

I apologise for murdering pandas and tigers.

I apologise that you'll never see the Amazon Rainforest.

I am sorry.

Arthur Hardy (12)

Knole Academy, Sevenoaks

Untitled

Education is fun,
I learn something every day.
Day after day,
I come to school dressed correctly,
Understanding new topics may be hard.

Maisie Caulfield (12)
Knole Academy, Sevenoaks

Time Ticking Away

When everything and anything become nothing,
What will you miss the most?
For freedom and peace are created by conflict's ghost.
When the time comes, those years become seconds,
And seconds tick, tick away.
Will you remember these days?
Will they just be a blank page?
No.
Why be a blank page?
Start from a clean slate,
Rewrite all the pain.
Stop counting down, stop watching the clock,
Stop wasting time, stop watching the sand drop.
Make memories out of moments you know will last
Start the trip to timelessness,
Lead a lightened path
Time is ticking away
So don't wait for a new day,
Say the words you want to say,
When the time comes, those years become seconds
And seconds tick life away.
Will you remember those days?
Yes, they were worth the wait.

Issie Williams (13)

Langley Park School For Girls, Beckenham

The Day Actually Came

I never thought this day would actually come,
I never thought I would be standing here talking to you,
I never thought I'd actually graduate.
To all the grad students, congrats,
I feel delighted to walk out here knowing all of you,
Knowing the wonderful things you have done.
These past four years have been the best,
Regardless of how it started, you've made it to the end.
Good and bad connections,
We've made friends along the way,
But I would say together we have a great bond,
The strongest.
People around you, whether you like it or not,
We have each other.
So, thank you for all the memories.
We may leave, going on to extraordinary things
But never the knowledge we learnt,
Or the love we share,
Or the battles we won,
Or the things we overcome.

Nimasin Jaiyesimi (13)
Langley Park School For Girls, Beckenham

Change Ignored

People are dying.
People are crying.
People are screaming.
People are preaching.
People are preaching to be better.
People are preaching for the worse.
You sit up on your throne of gold and ignore our cries.
You ignore our cries for better days.
You ignore our cries for help.
You ignore our cries for change.
You sit up on your throne of gold and watch us.
You watch us slowly die because of you.
You and your twisted lies.
Your lies are for the better.
Your lies for change.
You give us hope.
Then quickly take it away.
You take our hopes, our dreams away.

Alexandra Horrocks (12)
Langley Park School For Girls, Beckenham

Gold At The End Of The Tunnel

You're searching
Searching for the gold at the end of the tunnel
Digging down, down, down
You'll find it
Nobody believes you will
But you know it's there,
It's waiting
A voice from above calls
Diamonds! Diamonds! More than your gold
You drop the shovel
Climbing up, up, up
You look around at the waste left for you
Diamonds gone, maybe never there in the first place
Your gold cries out from under the shovel
It was closer than you thought
But now it's gone.

Sabrina Sharp (13)
Langley Park School For Girls, Beckenham

Success

Life is a battle,
You either fail or succeed,
So do something about it,
Life has given you opportunities,
So do something about it,
Don't just lie on your back and ignore your future,
It's all about the beginning of your story,
Don't worry about what you didn't do from the beginning,
Don't do it later, do it now,
Otherwise, it will be too late,
Even if you feel you can't do it,
Try, as we all make mistakes.

Ani Anaelova (13)
Langley Park School For Girls, Beckenham

Success Is The Best Version Of You

Cars drive by,
The birds are about to fly,
I see my future self,
Me and my future wealth,
You need to thrive,
Believe and strive,
Where do you *feel* most alive?
Success is the best version of you,
Don't let others hide or guide you,
Even when the times are rough,
You need to stand up, be tough,
For you, yourself,
For your future wealth,
Success is the best version of you,
And you should see that too.

Riya Naidoo (13)
Langley Park School For Girls, Beckenham

Love Yourself

B e happy

do **E** xciting things

L ove yourself

L ove others

you're **A** mazing

B e happy

b **E** the best version of yourself

L ive your life

L ove everyone

you're **A** mazing

do **T** hings that make you happy

E xplore your creativity

D on't worry about what others think

D o great things

Y ou are beautiful.

Bella Buttigieg (13)

Langley Park School For Girls, Beckenham

Friends Are Life

F riends are everything, friends are life.

R ise together, ride together.

I n every heart lives a friend or a couple, if you are lucky. In every friendship lives love.

E verything involves friends, everyone needs friends.

N ever say no one likes you; next to you is someone who does.

D ive into life together, diving always together, forever.

S afe is a feeling, safe is friends.

Ella Stewart (13)

Langley Park School For Girls, Beckenham

Be Yourself

Life is like a door,
Once you open it, it's full of opportunities,
But if you close it, the opportunities are gone,
So go for it, do whatever your heart desires,
And don't let anyone stop you,
You are you, that's enough,
Just be yourself!

It's all about the beginning of the story,
So give yourself the glory.

Thrive, drive and survive.

Sienna Austin (13)
Langley Park School For Girls, Beckenham

War

Why do we fight?
Can we try to find the light?
They give you life
Then you stab them with a knife
We talk about war
But can I not just enjoy a good s'more?
Everyone's dying
Or everyone is lying
They used to love
But now they're flying high with doves
Can we just start from the top
War must be put to a stop!

Millie Higgins (13)

Langley Park School For Girls, Beckenham

Equality

Each day, I am on a quest for equality.
Each day, I won't stop until my voice is heard.
Each day, I want to live better than my grandparents.
Each day, I want to make things better than I have.
Race, age, religion, we've got to be treated better
When equality is not unity's strife.

Gracie Banford

Langley Park School For Girls, Beckenham

Acting

A loud voice is key.
C onfidence, you need.
T ry and be yourself.
I nteract with the audience.
N ever give up.
G ive yourself to the stage.

You... have... got... this.

Poppy Dale (13)
Langley Park School For Girls, Beckenham

Free

Today: I feel sad
Today: I feel isolated
Today: I feel scared
Today: I feel depressed

One day: I will be happy
One day: I will be loved
One day: I will be free
One day: I will be me.

Grace Richardson (13)
Langley Park School For Girls, Beckenham

The Older Isn't Always The Wiser

I met my younger self, my inner child, at a café today.
Why though? You might ask.
It's because younger me was worried, so I asked her why.
She said that she had learned about climate in school,
And how she was getting scared.
She told me how the animals were dying and the plants were withering,
How she was angry with the adults who were meant to protect this planet,
How there was no second planet.
How this is our one and only home.

She talked about how paper straws, instead of plastic ones, still affected the planet,
And how it was not helping much at all.

I looked at her as tears were falling,
She was only so young, nine to be exact,
But she had been through so much,
And yet, after all this, she was ready to do what most people couldn't;
She was ready to speak up to tell people how they were wrong,
And make them change.

I looked through the window and thought about a few
things,
How humans had been the cause,
How the Great Australian Barrier Reef was dying,
And the LA fires, how that too had been our fault.
All of the droughts, fires, and rising sea levels had all been
the humans' fault.

I met up with my younger self in a café today,
And if I may say, it was the best thing that I may have done.
She opened my eyes to the harsh reality
In a way that others couldn't.

I met up with my younger self today,
Not to play,
But to change the world,
To change the planet,
To ensure that generations after us will thrive.

I met up with my younger self,
My inner child, at a café,
And now you know why.

Nora Nemes (13)
Swinton Academy, Mexborough

Oops...

The world's feeling hotter than an oven today,
Ice is melting fast. How is this okay?
We have made a massive accident, oops!
If we keep going this way, there will be no hope.
All of us must work together, can we go alone? Nope.
See, our planet is dying fast, with only us to blame,
But all of us are so uncaring when we should feel shame.
Come on, let us make a change, one for the better,
Now we need to act fast, stop the animal's pain.
We could do many things, like putting things in the recycling bins,
Or stop using plastic things.
We have made a massive accident, oops!
But right now, we can still easily fix it,
Let us all come together, and all of us do our bit.
While yes, climate change won't kill us for years,
But our laziness shouldn't be left to our grandchildren's fears.
Now, you may think these little things don't seem like much,
But if 8 billion of us do it, the world will be much cleaner,
Come and stop climate change, let's do it as a team.

Harry Phillips (12)
Swinton Academy, Mexborough

Pheasants Die When They Die

Out the cage door and up to the moor,
Looking up at the horizon to see the birds soar,
Through people's gardens and up winding roads,
And the fear of cars and garden gnomes,
But nothing compares to the sound of a leather hatch
unfolding to reveal a bullet shining and bold,
And how your life could end and the story untold,
And how the farmer could live life knowing of one that he
broke,
Upon the fields and the clatter of the tractor,
A friend and I, who joined me shortly after.
We dodge all cars and the garden gnomes,
And run between the gardens of people's homes,
And up to the moor,
To watch the birds soar.
But it all came to an end when a bullet penetrated his head,
No time to say goodbye as the bullet whispered his death,
Now I run, my eyes a blur and vision,
The smirk of the farmer's lips,
His life didn't matter, nor does mine,
As we are pheasants and we die when we die.

Charlotte Hampshire (12)

Swinton Academy, Mexborough

Maybe One Day

Maybe one day, people would be kinder,
Maybe one day, people wouldn't cut down trees,
Maybe one day, animals wouldn't be hurt by our actions,
Maybe one day, that could all change,
Maybe one day, people will care for the climate,
Maybe one day, our planet wouldn't be hurting,
Maybe one day, animal homes wouldn't be destroyed by
forest fires,
If only people cared.

Maybe one day it's time for us to step up,
Maybe one day it's time for us to make a change,
Maybe one day it's time for us to start now,
So we need to make a change,
And it needs to happen now.

If you really cared,
Why not help now?
The Earth is getting destroyed,
Time is running out,
Let's hope something happens soon,
Before our worst nightmares become reality.

Lola Oscroft (12)
Swinton Academy, Mexborough

Climate Change

C   arbon in the atmosphere increasing

L   ighting up the trees for roads and estates

I   ncreasing use of fossil fuels instead of renewable fuels

M   aybe if we all worked together we could stop it

A   ll of the trees will be chopped or burned

T   rees help us breathe, so we can't burn them and reuse carbon

E   veryone has to do their part.

C   limate change is becoming a climate emergency

H   ave you considered how you could stop it?

A   nimals like polar bears lose their habitats every day because of us

N   obody shouldn't try their best to help

G   reatness will be achieved if we overcome this great challenge

E   verybody should consider how to cut their carbon footprint.

Keyan Ebrahimi (13)
Swinton Academy, Mexborough

Confidence

C ome join in on games, don't feel left out! Be brave!

O pinions! Don't be scared to show your opinions in learning!

N ice! Be nice to people; don't be unkind, give them a smile!

F riends! Make friends. Don't be shy to ask people to be friends, it's not hard.

I get joined in, always! You need to have fun in school, while you can!

D ancing! Schools do competitions all the time in PE; get involved!

E agerness to be excited, but don't be annoying, it won't be fun!

N eedy! Don't be too needy, you can't get everything at once.

C onfidence - everyone needs this (everyone).

E xcitement; get excited, you will need the energy to get through this!

Scarlett Damms (11)

Swinton Academy, Mexborough

Empowerment

Empowerment isn't about being strong and it doesn't happen all at once.
It begins by taking small steps, raising your hand, asking questions, being resilient and trying again when it's hard.
It's the feeling that grows when you learn something new.
Being confident doesn't mean being right all the time, it means believing you can find the answers, it means showing up even when you're afraid.
Empowerment is not about being perfect, it is about being brave enough to face the challenges you come across.
Empowerment is finding the strength within yourself to grow, speak, shine and build your own path to walk on because you aren't walking down the same path as others.
Empowerment is using your voice to create your own story.

Liberty Munro (13)
Swinton Academy, Mexborough

Make The World A Better Place

The world needs to change,
Our planets come to shame.
The trees are dying,
Instead of multiplying.
The birds are crying,
Instead of them flying.
The pigs are screeching,
Instead of lovely oinking.
The orangutans are alone,
Instead of having a home.
The cows are now meat,
Instead of getting a treat.
The rhinos and elephants are losing their tusks,
To people who think they are a must.
Animals are going extinct,
Do humans even think?
People chopping trees,
Making it harder to breathe.
We hate destroying our planet,
So why is this becoming a habit?
Stop this madness,
Before we add on to this sadness.
Make this world a better place!

Mia Williams (13)
Swinton Academy, Mexborough

The Ever-So-Short And Depressing Life Of A Chicken

I saw a light,
A bright light, brighter than you've ever seen,
I heard people talking and even more chickens bawking,
I had just popped out of my egg,
However, it wasn't the farm I expected,
I expected to be able to see outside,
In a red barn with lots of sunshine,
Instead, it was dark, not much light at all,
I tried to walk around,
But I hit something metal,
I couldn't walk,
I couldn't flap,
I couldn't do anything,
I laid my first eggs,
And they were taken just a few seconds later,
Why am I here?
This is not a farm,
This is torture,
Then I was taken out,
Sent to the slaughterhouse.

Dylan Lee (12)
Swinton Academy, Mexborough

The Talking Lion

This chatty lion wants a friend
Will she have time?
One special lion asks a butterfly
It looks at the lion with fear and flies away
The lion anxiously asks a bee
Bee, could you be my friend?
The bee looks with horror, you'll eat me up
Maybe I need a stronger animal
She went to an alligator, you'll be greater
But you see, I'm in the sea
She went to an elephant, you'll be excellent
But the elephant is too giant
So she finds a mouse, but it's too small
Maybe life is best free, but as she says that, she finds a lion
Do you want to be friends?
We're a group anyway, but yes
True, true, and they stay in a friendship group.

Ivan Hopkinson (12)
Swinton Academy, Mexborough

What Has Our Generation Done?

What has our generation done?
From killing animals to destroying homes,
It seems like pollution has won.
We build factories and machines,
Thinking that it's fun.
However, what people don't realise
Is that climate change has come.
We need to act now,
Before it's too late...
Otherwise, this planet and us,
Are going to meet a hot, gruesome fate.

We try and try again,
Only for our results to be put to shame.
And all this time, whilst we're destroying this planet,
We're always asking... who is the one to blame?
People always ask, what have we become?
However, my question is, what has our generation done?

Randy Strauts (13)
Swinton Academy, Mexborough

The Eye Of An Eagle

Eagle, eagle, dance through the sky
Take flight at night, when no one can see.
Go hunting for food even if it puts up a fight.
Win this fight or go hungry.
Eagle, eagle, dance through the sky,
Don't let it out of your sight.
Dive and dodge through the trees, get your mouse.
Swoop in for the kill, aim it perfectly.
Eagle, eagle, go back to your tree,
To feed your family.
Feel proud and empowered.
Eagle, eagle, get some sleep,
Remember you are going to take off at night when no one
can see.
You will have to go hunting for food even if it puts up a
fight,
You do all this for your family, the one you love.
And always will.

Eve Houlbrook (12)
Swinton Academy, Mexborough

Our Twisted World

D angers of our children's and grandchildren's futures!
E mitting carbon into our saviour, the atmosphere.
F orests are losing their shine and nature.
O ur twisted, worthwhile animals are being murdered.
R ainforests becoming deserted,
E very day, slowly gets hotter.
S taying outside becomes a horror.
T he kids suffer and suffer.
A re we aiming for the end of us?
T rees give us our oxygen, keeping carbon down to size.
I ce caps melting, making our sea rise.
O r maybe we can just... do things to help?
N ow and only then can we have a good world.

Riley Miners (13)

Swinton Academy, Mexborough

Dolphin Of Death

Blood filled the ocean in a warm embrace,
Sharks swam towards the blood, for it had a great taste,
They swam, they swam with incredible haste,
A dolphin was bleeding – a lovely red paste.

The sharks attacked with a powerful bite,
They attacked the dolphin with a hateful spite,
But the dolphin resisted the urge to die,
It was in pain, but it didn't even cry.

The dolphin let out a ghastly shriek,
Although his chances of living were bleak,
He wounded the sharks with a very strong leap,
And the sharks let out a sad little weep.

Blood filled the ocean in a warm embrace,
But nothing swam towards the sharks' blood-red paste.

Jack Wheeler (12)
Swinton Academy, Mexborough

Making A Change

Beaneath one sun
We are all born
To skies of blue and fields of corn
Yet storms now rage and forests fall
A silent cry that echoes all
The oceans full with plastic
While glaciers weep the species hide
The Earth, once vast with breath
But justice too must find its place in every land
For how we can protect the trees
Where hate and power rule below
To heal the world we must all unite together
Be guarded by a world that is fair
So rise we must
With hands placed together
With open hearts and sharpened minds
The Earth we share is not for the few
Its fate is ours
And ours to renew.

Elizabeth Hewitson (13)
Swinton Academy, Mexborough

In My Dreams

In my dreams, I wish that the world was not damaged or slowly dying,
But that's just a dream.
In my dreams, I hope that animals aren't harmed in a way of getting killed for no reason,
But that's just a dream.
But maybe it doesn't have to be 'just a dream',
In my dreams, I wish that people aren't so cruel they would hunt an animal just for fun or making smoke from cigarettes that kill the environment,
Because of all the damage we have done to our planet,
We have killed over forty-two million per day,
But in my dreams I wish that our planet was back to normal...
Nobody can change my dreams...

Flick Martin (12)
Swinton Academy, Mexborough

Silent Serpent

Slippery, slithery serpent,
Coiling in a quiet fight,
Venom oozes from jagged fangs,
Its scales reflect the fading light.
It creeps with an eerie, silent glide,
To challenge a hawk that swoops down with pride,
A sudden strike, a flash of fear,
It leaves behind the dead and a baby deer.
A horse once trotting through the field,
Now silent, lifeless, fate sealed.
From out of a deep, shadowed lair,
It slithers forth at a ruthless speed,
The storm surrounds its every move,
A creature driven by its greed.
The snake found a mouse resting beneath a stone,
One bite, and it is left alone.

Alfie Dungworth (12)
Swinton Academy, Mexborough

Swam

Deep in the ocean
The shark swam in what looked like slow motion
Drifting aimlessly about
And in his mind there was not a doubt

As the shark stalked his prey
It realised it did not want the stingray
Nor the octopus
Nor the squid
But some fish would make a tasty dish

And in the depths of the murky waters
There were some fish just waiting to be slaughtered
The shark licked its lips
It was going to make a meal of this.

So as the shark opened its jaw
He ate, but realised - this was such a bore
So back to his home he went
With his time not well spent.

Evie Birkbeck (12)

Swinton Academy, Mexborough

Snap Your Fingers, And Change

If you could snap your fingers and change one thing,
What would you change?
I would change everything.
I would change that we cut and burn down our trees,
The trees that feed us, cure us, give us oxygen.
I would change our factories,
That pollute our air, make us sick.
I would snap my fingers and give back the homes
To the animals that lost them.
If you didn't snap your fingers and change this,
We would just end up like them.
We would not have our home back.
So, one last time, I have to say:
If you could snap your fingers and change something...
What would you change?

Olivia Allott (13)

Swinton Academy, Mexborough

Eagle Of The Night

The eagle cries as the wind whistles around its wings,
Fastest bird of the day and night.
Its beak sharp as a knife, the eagle strikes again,
Fly, fly through the fight, seek adventure after day and night.
Fly, fly in the sky, how does it feel to be so high?
Biggest bird in the sky, biggest wings of them all,
Eagle, eagle, of the night, how do you fly so high?
Danger, danger after dawn, danger, danger you cause.
Eagle, eagle, of the night, craves the thrill of the fight,
Dive, dive at the eagle's strike.
The eagle enjoys the fight,
All day, all night, the eagle stalks its prey.

Finley Newton (12)
Swinton Academy, Mexborough

Me, Myself And I In The World

I am in the world,
I am in the grass,
I am in the trees,
I am in every woman and man,
I am in the seas.
I see myself in everything,
Including the gentle breeze.
I see myself in the gleam of the moon,
As well as the radiance of the sun.
As well as the clouds and the pitter-patter of the falling raindrops,
I am also in the droughts,
The people who drown,
Every sorrow and doubt,
Every death,
Every storm,
Every tear,
Every failure,
And every fear that radiates from everyone.
I feel everything everyone else feels, and together, we are an Iron Fist.

Leila Stephens (13)
Swinton Academy, Mexborough

Sharky Shark

Deep in the ocean
Cold and almost frozen
Bobda the Great White
Looked to fill fish with great fright
Soon enough, a school of fish swam by
Above, a fisherman was eating pie
Bobda lurked in the shadows
Her belly bellowed
She swam on the seabed
Looking to eat a fish head
Soon one popped out
Bit the pole and the fisherman shouted
Bobda took her chance
And struck the fish with force, so it wobbled the fisherman's hand
That was her tea
In the massive sea
But one problem
She got her mouth stuck
And it wouldn't open.

Will Kelly (11)
Swinton Academy, Mexborough

Football

F orlán
O penda
O doffin
T evez
B ellingham
A dama Traoré
L eo Messi
L amine Yamal
E usébio
R onaldo

F rankfurt
O xford
O lympica
T ottenham Hotspur
B ournemouth
A l-Nassr
L iverpool
L eeds
E xeter City
R eal Madrid

These players and teams are as fast as Usain Bolt,
As strong as bodybuilders,
And win games like they are playing against five-year-olds.

Hasan Bilyal (11)
Swinton Academy, Mexborough

Human Ignorance

The trees come crashing down, their faces now a frown,
Their desperate cries for help,
Drowned out in the distant yelps,
Their bodies are now limp, as their habitat starts to shrink,
Their frantic scrambling away, and yet the people continue
their stay,
Destruction seems their passion, turning animal skins into
fashion,
The machines churn and growl; their whole situation is foul,
If we want to end up dead, complete this continuous thread,
This thread of death and destruction, or follow my
instructions,
Keep this world alive, if you want to continue to thrive.

Jessica Hampshire (13)
Swinton Academy, Mexborough

Climate

Yo, yo, yo, yo, yo, got you on with the pick
And roll climate change ain't sicko mode
Boom, boom, boom, boom, boom

The ice caps are melting real fast
We need the polar bears to last

Yo, yo it's Zaynab, my country's mother
Joining hot, now I'm in Leeds
But in Somaliland we have no weeds
Straight desert fam

Yo, yo, it's Omar the orangutan
Crowd goes wild
Yo, yeah I was swinging through the trees
With my mate Pete
Now no one can compete
'Cause my bro Pete is now...

Palm oil.

George Saunders (13)
Swinton Academy, Mexborough

A Destroyed World

Climate change, a world crisis.
This has been going on for some years now
Yet nothing is being done about it.
Trees are getting chopped down
And animals that live in them
Are getting their homes destroyed.
Trees give us oxygen,
The more we chop down,
The less oxygen we will have
Unless animals will have homes.
Speaking of animals,
Animals are getting hunted for food.
Some are near the point of extinction.
We need to do something about climate change
Before we can't.
The world isn't a resource, it's our home.

Jax Adkins (13)
Swinton Academy, Mexborough

Future

One day, there'll be no planet to call our own,
If every day our progress is being blown,
Day by day, the trees are falling;
All of the nature we take for granted,
It's appalling.

The sea levels continue to rise, as we watch
Mesmerised by our mistakes.

The animals keep losing their homes, and the future
Generations will be all alone.

It is getting too late, only we can't decide our fate
Before it can't be saved or there'll be
No animals
No towns
No people
No future.

Franceska Woolley (13)
Swinton Academy, Mexborough

Help Our Earth

The planet is dying
Are we even trying?
We need to help our precious Earth, instead of making it worse
We are chopping trees and not using them to breathe
Animals are going extinct,
Did you even think?
Homes are getting destroyed
Making all the animals paranoid
The trees are dying instead of multiplying
Animals need homes, so why are we making them unknown?
We make dogs pets,
So why are we making other animals our food next?
We are all walking the streets
Not knowing what's going to happen next week...

Ellie Line (13)
Swinton Academy, Mexborough

The Lion's Fight

Lion, Lion, in the night,
Runs through the trees, looking for a fight,
Lion, Lion slits your throat,
Watches you cry, "Help me! Help me!"
Lion, Lion witnesses you die,
Because it's too late now,
You've lost this fight,
Lion, Lion brings you to his lair,
This isn't fair,
But you don't dare,
You should have won,
But now it's done,
Lion, Lion, in the night,
Lion, Lion, starved last night,
Lion, Lion shall feast tonight,
Because Lion, Lion has won the fight.

Rose Bradley (11)
Swinton Academy, Mexborough

What Are We Doing?

C utting down forests
L oss of habitat for animals
I ncreasing reports of extreme weather
M ore and more threat to society
A nimals being killed for ourselves
T he sea's water level is rising
E xpanding urbanisation.

C O2 building up in the atmosphere
H eat rising rapidly
A nimals becoming extinct
N ext generations let down
G reenhouse gas emissions heating planet
E veryone still does nothing.

Ross Mitchell (12)

Swinton Academy, Mexborough

Football Teams

F ernandes shoots like a rocket zooming through the air,

O degaard's stamina is like a gazelle,

O bi's height is like a giraffe reaching for food in the trees,

T rent Alexander-Arnold passes the ball like it's nothing,

B ellingham is as strong as a gorilla,

A mad Diallo runs like a cheetah chasing its food,

L amine Yamal dribbles through the team like it's nothing,

L ionel Messi - small and quiet as a mouse, but as great as a lion.

Jamie Lawless (12)
Swinton Academy, Mexborough

Invisible Smoke

The dot date is near
There's not much time left
Tigers wailing in desperation
We dream of an epiphany
A blessing from the sky
That we can erase our damage
But we've done enough now
It's almost irreversible
Let's gather
One by one
People by people
Group by group
Country by country
Continent by continent
A world of all
We know all too well we've done this
Stop the invisible smoke
Stop hiding
Speak out soon
Alert the issue.

Ted Morgan (13)
Swinton Academy, Mexborough

Change Needs To Happen

C hange needs to happen,
L ittering destroys the planet,
I s this reality?
M any homes lost,
A nimals losing lives,
T rees being cut down for paper,
E ventually, the planet will die.

C hange needs to happen,
H abitats disappearing,
A n environment ruined,
N obody willing to help the change,
G et ready to get up and help,
E verybody, put our heads together and make this a better place.

Millie Hamshaw (13)
Swinton Academy, Mexborough

Change

I open up my window,
And see nothing at all, just fumes of smoke galore.
I miss the birds chirping,
It's not the same when the men are working.
I miss the crashing of the waves,
But I haven't heard them for days.
The world is getting hotter each day,
What can I say?
I can speak about climate change to everyone who's around,
Even though the people can't always be found.
With your help, we can stop the crime,
And hopefully save it in time.

Summer North (12)

Swinton Academy, Mexborough

Joy

The breeze once whispered through the trees,
A lullaby upon the seas,
The coral danced in colours bright,
The world was full of pure delight.

But now the winds are fierce and dry,
The oceans drown, the forests die,
The colours fade, the sky turns grey,
And all the joy is washed away...

We need to help, we need to think,
Before our towns and cities sink,
It's our problem we need to solve,
To keep our Earth healthy for us all.

Nicola Tomasiewicz (13)
Swinton Academy, Mexborough

Imagine It Was You

Imagine it was you.
Your home gone.
Your family dead.
Imagine it was you.
Watching everything you used to have
Being stolen from you.
Being turned into waste and plastic,
And even shampoo.
Imagine it was your home,
Torn down and ruined.
Before you hurt more,
Stop and think about what you're doing.
Now imagine it was you and take a minute.
If you don't stop now,
The world is finished.

Hollie Backhouse (13)
Swinton Academy, Mexborough

Nature's Not On Their Side

Nature's not on their side,
In 100 years, all animals could die,
In this heat, they could fry,
Or deforestation could kill them off.

Nature's not on their side,
Daily they're struggling to survive,
Can you not hear their cries,
So why not help these poor creatures?

Nature's not on their side,
So why don't you stop their cries,
And help them survive?
Now's the time.

Danny Allwood (12)
Swinton Academy, Mexborough

Our Future

Do you remember me?
I'm you,
I am very different,
I'm dying,
We are killing ourselves,
By killing our planet,
Habitats are being destroyed,
Animals stranded,
Biodiversity gone,
All our medicine, food,
And so much more,
You can help,
But there's always an excuse,
You need to help, have to,
The littlest thing,
Can change everything,
So you can change everything!

Mia Glossop (13)
Swinton Academy, Mexborough

Watch Out, There's A Wolf!

Wolf, wolf, fierce growl,
Beady eyes and sharp claws,
This wolf is as hard as nails.
Watch out, here they come,
As sly as can be,
The grey fur as thick as clumps.
Wolf, wolf with sharp, shiny teeth,
Stalk the humans in the dark.
Sneaking quietly while they wait,
Watch out, here they come.
Pounce quietly on the prey,
Stay quiet before they hear.
Do you fear the wolf?

Lily Beardsley (12)
Swinton Academy, Mexborough

It's Too Late

The buildings are tall
The cars keep driving
People go to work
People do as they like
No one sees the change
No one sees the smoke
The sky turns black
The sun disappears
No one sees the change
The creatures in the forest run away
The creatures disappear
No one sees the change
The city grows larger
The forests get smaller
No one sees the change
The world is changing
But no one will notice until it's too late.

Scarlett Cantrell (13)
Swinton Academy, Mexborough

Elephants In The Jungle

E lephants stomping around
L iving in the jungle; that's where they're found
E lephants squirting water at their prey
P iles of fruit that they eat every day
H iding in the trees, but they're easily found
A nd their ears are so big and round
N ot very small, they are very big
T hey loom over the monkeys, capybaras, and pigs.

Charlie Addy (12)
Swinton Academy, Mexborough

We're Killing The Earth

We're killing the Earth,
And that's not fun.
Our oceans are dying,
And no one will help.
The world is getting hotter by every second,
And it's because of us.
They're burning down all the trees,
And no one seems to care.
At this point, we aren't going to make it,
To the year 2040.
All of our creatures are dying,
And soon you'll be crying.

Rose Outram (13)
Swinton Academy, Mexborough

The King Of The Jungle

The King Cobra - the king of the jungle,
And your mind,
Whilst hidden beneath the leaves,
Your mortal eyes cannot see the beast,
It's graceful yet strong,
The sleek body made of 100% muscle,
From cannibalisation to killing elephants,
You can't control what the king does,
Fear will haunt you, and it will kill you,
So don't underestimate the king of the jungle.

Cameron Willis (12)
Swinton Academy, Mexborough

Creature Of The Night

I stroll in the night
Looking left and right
I am free
So don't come and rescue me
The wind pushes my fur back
When the sky turns black
I am happy as ever, catching my prey
Every day
I howl at the moon
My eyes sparkling in the night
I turn to my right
And that's where I take flight.
What am I?

Answer: I am a wolf of terror.

Millie Fenton-Wightman (11)
Swinton Academy, Mexborough

Rainforest Dying

R ainforest thriving
A ll animals surviving
I n the forest that's dying
N obody cares
F or the animals in despair
O rangutans burning
R are to see animals surviving
E verybody doesn't know the rainforest is dying
S o when tigers are extinct
T hink about the rainforest that was once thriving.

Matty Beckitt (12)
Swinton Academy, Mexborough

Climate Change

C   arbon footprint
L   ittering
I   mpact on the future
M   aking more factories
A   nimal testing
T   aking sea animals to eat
E   nvironment.

C   utting down trees
H   urting nature for our benefit
A   nimals are losing their habitats
N   ever stopping
G   as
E   lectricity.

Lois Cooke (13)
Swinton Academy, Mexborough

Untitled

Furious, fast, fierce, the tiger is not scaled to bite.
And after seen, most people are lost with a fright.
These creatures are normally sent to the zoo,
Because of how cool they are, they send shivers down people's spines.
Their sharp teeth could kill you so keep a look out,
Because they are very fast.
It's safe to say lions aren't to be messed with.

Isacc Thorpe (11)
Swinton Academy, Mexborough

Dying Flower

She describes herself as a dying flower
A bad weather day
Wanting to change fast like the weather
But never does
Instead, she's feeling like climate change
Long, slow, and bad
A dying flower doesn't feel loved
A bad weather day doesn't feel enjoyed
The climate change has changed
So why couldn't she change into a loved flower?

Chloe Hatfield (13)
Swinton Academy, Mexborough

Climate Change

C arbon footprints
L and under water
I ll-minded people
M illions of years for nothing
A mazon desert
T rees to fuel
E cosystems gone

C arbon is the new oxygen
H eated too much
A ll life is dead
N o more ice
G lobal warming
E xtinction.

Bodhi Connolly (12)
Swinton Academy, Mexborough

Climate Change

C   arbon footprint
L   ittering
I   mpact on the future
M   aking more factories
A   nimals losing their habitats
T   aking habitats
E   nvironment.

C   utting down trees
H   unting animals for their tusks
A   nimal testing
N   o trees
G   as
E   lectricity.

Emily Hampshire (12)
Swinton Academy, Mexborough

The Wild Elephant

The grateful elephant wandered,
Wandered it did,
Bang!
A powerful shot rang out through the air,
The scared elephant ran,
Ran and ran,
Bang!
Another shot into the air,
The unstoppable elephant was stopped,
Poor elephant,
Poor,
Poor,
Elephant,
It's not easy to make a difference,
The poor elephant tried,
So should everyone.

Noah Bennett (12)
Swinton Academy, Mexborough

Slaughterhouse

Cunning little creature creeps round corners.
He sees paintings of seas.
He shoots through rooms with chickens.
He was moving swiftly, deafening, getting away from the slaughters.
He never knew what his destiny would be.
As he was running as rapidly as he could.
He didn't know his fortune would lead him to this.
The meat grinder.

Eva Whike-Blunt (12)
Swinton Academy, Mexborough

All About Football

F   antastic footwork with the ball
O   vercome your dreams of scoring a goal
O   utshine the haters
T   ransfer to the team you love
B   alance on your feet, dribbling on the pitch
A   drenaline runs through the players
L   earn to perform in front of everyone
L   ove the fans chanting your name.

Toby Phillips (12)

Swinton Academy, Mexborough

Climate Change

Factories smoking
Rubbish rolling
Stop! Stop! Stop!
Humans change
Not
Climate change
Animals dying
Trees crying
Stop! Stop! Stop!
Trees stay
Rubbish goes away
Engines roaring
Water pouring
Climate
Go away!
End climate change!
Help the Earth
Let the world live
Without pain!

Ayla Nuttall (12)
Swinton Academy, Mexborough

I Believe

I believe that the world is changing
I believe we need to change
I believe we are losing animals
I believe it's climate change
I believe the ice is melting
I believe the sea is rising
I believe the fish are going
I believe houses are going with floods
I believe it's heating up
I believe we need to change.

Thomas Meggitt (13)
Swinton Academy, Mexborough

Untitled

A red panda it is,
A red panda, it says,
Dear panda, are you okay?
A red panda is quiet,
It doesn't cause any riot.
Though it is endangered,
For whatever reason they favour.
It is rarely seen,
As it's usually in the trees.
They chew bamboo,
And go on a walk,
But they never really talk.

Mena Claiyapartho (12)
Swinton Academy, Mexborough

Echoes Of Ruin

The cities where the towers stood tall,
Now whispers of a sheltered call,
The Earth, once lush,
Now cracked and dry.
Beneath a dim and smoky sky.

We built with hands, yet tore apart,
The very world that held our heart,
Now silent regions where voices cried,
As nature's tears are left to hide.

Harriett Clarke (12)
Swinton Academy, Mexborough

Climate

C limate
L ittering
I ce melting
M inor care
A busing species
T oday's Earth
E arth dying

C aring less
H unting animals
A nimals dying
N eeding shelter
G laciers melting
E nd the suffering.

Lewis Hawley (12)
Swinton Academy, Mexborough

Fire Is Burning

Fires are burning, habitats destroyed.
Less and less oxygen.
By day, plants burnt to a crisp,
Plants dying,
Animals dying.
Stop the fires before the oxygen levels drop,
And more black smoke is released into the air.
Fires are taking over nature,
Help stop the forest fires before it's too late.

Ruby Grocott (13)
Swinton Academy, Mexborough

Climate Change Isn't A Game

C hange now
L ife ends
I nternet chaos
M ake up
A fter all
T ime isn't forever
E nding is now

C hange time
H appy ending
A fter time it
N ever ends
G ames equal chaos
E nd climate change.

Lorelai Jones-Lee (13)
Swinton Academy, Mexborough

The Future

Dear future me, will there be any polar bears?
Will there be any turtles left from pollution?
Maybe in my dreams, there will,
The world needs to change,
There is too much stuff happening,
It needs to stop,
Clean up the litter,
Clean up the seas,
And keep the trees,
Do it for our generation.

Ashton-Lewis Kennedy (13)
Swinton Academy, Mexborough

Climate Change

C lubbing
L osing species
I mprovisation footprint
M ovement
A nti-climate change
T rees
E lectricity.

C lubbing
H elping climate change
A ctivist
N o trees
G reenhouse gases
E lectricity.

Joey Garner (12)
Swinton Academy, Mexborough

Football

Football is addicting,
It fills me with adrenaline,
It makes me feel seen,
It hand-picked a community for me.
It gave me an outlet for stress,
It's given me confidence, friendships, happiness,
And it gave me motivation to be the best me,
And the most important is it makes me feel... empowered!

Halli Beckett (11)
Swinton Academy, Mexborough

Football

F ancy footwork by the players,
O verlooked players beamed,
O ut come the haters,
T eams fight for promotion
B all flying at the speed of light,
A drenaline pushes through players,
L oving fans support the teams,
L ovely play fight for the teams.

Seth Rouane (12)
Swinton Academy, Mexborough

My Ozzie Owl

Owl, owl
In the sky, what's
It like to be so high,
Staring down on your prey,
Are you going to kill them today?

In the dark, in the dark
Where you stay?
The glow in your eyes
Brightens the day
Your wings spread so wide
In the night
I like to say
Goodnight.

Jack Hirst (12)
Swinton Academy, Mexborough

Our World

Our planet is very big, it has water, trees, light and life.
It was beautiful, calm and quiet, but then something came,
it was a human.
First, it started cutting down trees, then it started killing
innocent animals and burning fossil fuels.
Now, all that is left is just a big, hellish pit.
Nothing is left.

Charlie Johnson (12)
Swinton Academy, Mexborough

Be Strong

I feel a fire inside of me,
A strength I didn't know I had.
With courage, I can do anything.
And move past my fears.

Every step makes me feel stronger,
And I believe in myself.
Being empowered means I can shine,
And be proud of who I am.
No one or anything can stop me now!

Olivia Horner (13)
Swinton Academy, Mexborough

Football

F ootball is full of fancy footwork
O nly the best can pull it off
O vercome all the hate
T ransfer to the team you love
B alance on the pitch and dribble
A drenaline rush in my blood
L earn from your mistakes
L ead and conquer.

Jack Garrett (13)
Swinton Academy, Mexborough

Untitled

Corolla - a decent pace, crazy car
Rolls-Royce - a beautiful beast
Aston Martin - an old yet gold
Zaz - an amazing automobile
Yaris - a new but fast car
Corvette - a spectacular supercar
Acura - cool crazy car
Rav - an off-road beast
Suzuki - a joyful Japanese car.

Harley Hale (12)
Swinton Academy, Mexborough

The Hunter Panther

Panther, panther, the best hunter
Animals are scared of him
He can camouflage in
The dark, like a shadow.

P redator
A gility
N atural camouflage
T actical hunter
H unter
E liminates prey
R eady to attack.

Nevin Roby (12)
Swinton Academy, Mexborough

Lion, Lion

Lion, Lion, with your fur so bright,
Just like the sun burning bright,
With your eyes so light,
Your body takes flight,
Lion, Lion, stalking your feast,
Ready to approach your deadly feast,
Lion, Lion, with your roar so loud,
It makes your enemies follow the crowd.

Evie Harris (12)
Swinton Academy, Mexborough

Earth Is Drowning

Please help pull the plug,
You can't think straight when drowning,
Neither can the Earth.

Colonies are dying,
But caught up in city life,
People turn blind eyes.

It is not too late,
We can all still do something,
Please help save the Earth.

Jake Beardsley (13)
Swinton Academy, Mexborough

The Flamingo

F laming hot pink.
L eaping on its rubbery feet.
A ligned with the sky.
M oving its head softly.
I dentical to the bloomy blossoms.
N eon pink feathers.
G liding on its feet.
O rnamental in glory.

Freya Atkin (12)
Swinton Academy, Mexborough

Climate Change

The world needs to change
In order to stop climate change
Trees are dying
Trees are burning
Ashes to ashes
Dust to dust
The pollution is a problem
We need to stop this!
What can you do?
Let's work together
To change this!

Mineda Milasauske (13)
Swinton Academy, Mexborough

Cheetahs

C heetahs have rights
H orrendously they're trapped in cages
E xcellent cats of the wild
E xtremely fast
T ough creatures
A ll around the world
H ard to catch
S eriously difficult to see.

Pippa Mitchell (12) & Scarlett
Swinton Academy, Mexborough

Oxygen

O xygen helps us to survive
X avier is breathing because of trees
Y oung boy loves to study oxygen
G reggory died due to bad lungs and no oxygen
E ven with trees there is not enough air
N obody can outrun oxygen.

Kaylum Donnelly-Dodd (12)

Swinton Academy, Mexborough

Destruction Is Progress?

Destruction is progress?
Homes ripped from innocent animals' grasp.
Destruction is progress?
Lives stolen, loved ones gone.
Destruction is progress?
Just ask yourself, take a moment to think...
This destruction is... 'progress'?

Charlotte Wilcock (12)
Swinton Academy, Mexborough

A Dead Pigeon

The town was quiet,
But later in the day, it was like a riot,
People everywhere; left, right, front and centre,
Some people are having a bit of banter.
No one notices a pigeon that has been trampled on.
Guess what its name is? It's John.

Alfie Stark (12)
Swinton Academy, Mexborough

Electric Go-Karting

G ood for fun and laughter
O ut in the world of racing

K ing of the track
A in't no one beating me!
R ace me round all the circuits and watch me win
T urn on the electricity! Watch me go!

Bradley Horner (13) & Jake
Swinton Academy, Mexborough

Features Of A Lionfish

L ittle but brave
I gnorant to other fish
O range as the sun
N ice if unharmed
F eared by humans
I ntimidating to other friends
S piky like a hedgehog
H ides in the rocks.

Harrison Yarrow (11)
Swinton Academy, Mexborough

Save The Trees And Animals

Most animals die from one another, but not from humans.
Most trees decay, but not from humans.
The trees come down, and the orangutans are not found.
Maybe one day, the animals aren't harmed,
Maybe one day, the trees will be calm.

Charley-Jo Rickson (13)
Swinton Academy, Mexborough

The Mysterious Cheetah

C reeping up on its prey
H astily it strays away
E ating animals
E liminating diagonals
T rying to capture different prey
A nimals, what can I say?
H e knows they just want to stay.

Connor Swift (11)
Swinton Academy, Mexborough

Confidence

C ourage
O pen communication
N ever give up
F amily and friends
I ndependent
D ecisions
E njoy life
N ever say no
C oncentrate
E ncourage.

Gracie-Mai White (12)
Swinton Academy, Mexborough

The Terrifying Tremendous Tiger

T igers' fur so gold, even
I f they grow old,
G rass is where they lie,
E ven if they like to find prey,
R aw meat is what they eat. They're always on their feet.

Niamh Higham (11)
Swinton Academy, Mexborough

Untitled

Rodger, Rodger, burning on a road,
Who would dare to run over a poor cat.
Poor Rodger looking like honey on a baking tray.
While Jamie is flooding his house with tears,
And Dad blaming it on Sunya.

Matthew Harrop (12)
Swinton Academy, Mexborough

Excellent Elephants

As tall as a building,
As scary as the sea,
As strong as a wall,
As intelligent as robots,
As old as time,
As powerful as can be,
As unstoppable as a villain,
Excellent elephants.

Grayson Abbott (12)
Swinton Academy, Mexborough

Lion Lying Lightly

Lion lying lightly,
Stalking his feast.
Lion lying lightly,
His eyes burn brightly.
Lion lying lightly,
His body is so bossy.
Lion lying lightly,
Who will see your light?

Orla Gannon (11)
Swinton Academy, Mexborough

The Lion's Eye

The lion's roar was as loud as a train's horn,
Around the corner was its prey,
Walking slowly, sneakily towards its prey,
It jumped as far as it could,
The lion had a feast.

Dionne Kesse-Oware (11)

Swinton Academy, Mexborough

The Forest

Running that fast, I forgot the past
Everything flashed past me as I sprinted through the forest
My fierce eyes burned into my prey's eyes
I sprinted past the desert into the forest.

Olivia Birch (12)

Swinton Academy, Mexborough

The Vibrant Orange Tiger

T eeth as sharp as a knife
I gnite the night
G rey piercing eyes
E ating recklessly, tearing apart its quarry
R estless nights hunting its prey.

Summer Whitehead (12)
Swinton Academy, Mexborough

Climate Change

The trees are ruined
The fire is brewing
The orangutans are failing
And the palm oil is staining
Stop climate change
The killers need to be framed!

Darcie Watkins (12)

Swinton Academy, Mexborough

Climate, Climate, Climate

Ice is melting quicker than an ice cube,
People are hurting the animals with a lot of attitude.
Climate, climate, climate,
Why do we do this?

Tommy Dudley (13)
Swinton Academy, Mexborough

Climate Change

Land cleared, buildings appeared
Animals gone, death begun
Trees died, and leaves have fled
Internet is turned on, and scrolling goes on.

Annabelle Young (13)
Swinton Academy, Mexborough

Everything You Need To Know About Me

Likes to fish
Loves to game
Hates social times
But wants fame
Kind of thick
No tricks
Hates people.

Tayla Shaw (12)
Swinton Academy, Mexborough

Tim The Turtle

There once was a turtle called Tim
But Tim wanted to swim
But Tim's tank was too slim.

Logan Bennett (12)
Swinton Academy, Mexborough

Reading Empowers Me

I opened up a lovely book,
A whisper waiting in a nook.
Soon, the words were in my head,
They lit a spark and boldly said,
"You have a story to be told."

The pages turned,
My world grew wide,
Until I'd lived a thousand lives.
Within a book,
Inside my little reading nook.

When I am reading, I am not just me,
I hold the ring, I face the dark,
Like Frodo,
Brave, just with a spark.

I cast a spell at Hogwarts' gate,
With Hermione's mind and Harry's fate.
I climb through wardrobes, cold and white,
With Lucy's hope and Aslan's light.

I race with Katniss through the trees,
A bow and arrow, wind and leaves.
The capital won't see me fall,
I rise again, I risk it all.

When I am reading,
I become a hundred voices,
Not just one.
So if you ask me who I am,
I'm Bilbo, Meg and Peter Pan.
I'm every tale I've ever known,
And reading makes that strength my own.

Frankie Wilkins (12)
Tettenhall College, Tettenhall

Exams

Stress can be triggered
Of what trigger does your level have?
My stress is triggered by exams
Exams are hard, tests are hard

I have anxiety, I have mental health
Most of all, I have no off switch for my brain
My brain doesn't know when to turn off and relax
I think of bad things, I think of mental abuse
I think about judgement.

Up to exams, and I overthink, I struggle
With thoughts of the other subjects
I struggle about what happens if I get home and fail
An inspiring person told me otherwise
They told me that I can do so much more
So what if you aren't accidentally smart
You might be other things, smart.

Don't give up
Don't overpower your stress level,
You are capable of anything.

Zara Purchase (12)
Tettenhall College, Tettenhall

My Sisters, My Strength

Lola laughs loud and lifts the room's light,
With a heart that hugs and eyes shining bright.
Maddison's steady, strong like the sea,
Always the calm and the courage in me.

Lissy's a spark - wild, warm and free,
She dances through life, inspiring me.
And Mila, the sweetest, a joy so pure,
With every smile, I'm stronger, for sure.

Each one a piece of who I've become,
My sisters, my circle, my unbreakable sum.
We shout, we cry, we dream, we play,
But love leads us, come what may.

They stand beside me when I feel small,
Catch every stumble, answer each call.
With them, I rise, no need to pretend -
My sisters, my heroes, my lifelong best friends.

Lily Stonehouse (12)
Tettenhall College, Tettenhall

This Is Me!

Maybe your friends are good at art,
Maybe they're good at sports.
Maybe they have good fashion sense,
Maybe they are popular.
Maybe you don't know what you're good at,
Maybe you want to be like them,
But you're not them.

You may not be good at the things they're good at,
But you're good at being you.
But what else am I good at?

Am I good at being kind?
Am I good at being unique?
Am I good at looking after people?
Am I good at making people feel better?
Am I good at caring for animals?
Am I good at listening?
Am I a good person?

I am who I am,
And I'm not going to change.
This is me!

Honey Smith (12)
Tettenhall College, Tettenhall

My Dream

When I was young, what did I want to be?
A poet, a baker, or something easy.
When I was young, I heard the same question,
How would you earn this job?
Someone give me a suggestion!
Should I push through life and become something big,
Or should I stay away from fame and be happy with how I live?

I'm now older and I have a big dream,
I'm going to push myself 'til I succeed.
I want to sing on stage and write my own songs,
I want to be happy with my family, be happy with what I've got.

But for now, I'm happy and I'm strong,
I'll make my family happy, and make it last for long.

Mia Kearns (12)
Tettenhall College, Tettenhall

I Am Empowered

I know I can, I know I will,
Even when the world is still.
I've got ideas, I've got a voice,
And every day I make a choice.

To learn, to grow, to try my best,
To stand up tall and face each test.
When things go wrong, I don't give in -
I take a breath and try again.

I'm not alone - there's help around,
In every book, in every sound.
My teachers, friends, and family, too,
They help me see what I can do.

Empowered means I'm strong inside,
With dreams to chase and steps to guide.
I may be young, but I believe,
There's nothing that I can't achieve.

Arjun Kahlon (12)

Tettenhall College, Tettenhall

The Realisation

I thought football would lead the way,
A dream that would take me far.
At Wolves Academy, I would play,
And rise like a shooting star.

At school, I didn't do my best,
Because I thought I'd just be fine.
Why study hard? I'll pass the test,
Football will make me shine.

But now I know it's not enough,
One dream can't carry me through.
I need a plan if things get tough,
A backup plan to see me through.

Football's my dream, it always has been,
Studying hard, giving my best.
I'll work hard, on and off the scene,
In the future, I must now invest.

Elia Jackson (12)
Tettenhall College, Tettenhall

They Can

They play sports,
They go running,
They are athletic,
They are winning.

They can hike to a peak,
They can swim underwater.
There are two languages they can speak,
There's no challenge for others.

They want to drive a car,
They want to go far,
They want to rule the world,
They want to have control.

But what about me?
I can't ride a bike or juggle bowling pins,
I can't do a magic trick or make the world spin.
So I sit under my tree,
Writing about others, for a writer I shall be.

Harvey Westwood-Hilbert (12)
Tettenhall College, Tettenhall

Beyond The Surface

Your appearance and looks are not what define you,
People come in different shapes and sizes too.
From the colour of your hair to the sizes of your shoes,
There is nothing to be ashamed of for just being you.
The most amazing friends come from the most unlikely places,
Friends that, no matter what, have smiles on their faces.
Friends are the ones who don't want you to change,
The ones who remind you that nothing's out of range
Through thick and thin, through high and low,
Your family is by your side, no matter where you go.

Nevaeh Jackson (12)
Tettenhall College, Tettenhall

Noodles

A different flavour every time,
Some spicy pot noodles in your mouth,
Tingly sensation all around,
Looking at them in the hot water,
Imagine savouring them on your tongue.

A different flavour every time,
A squishy boiled egg making your mouth water,
The explosion of taste from the soup,
Then you slurp the long noodles into your mouth.

A different flavour every time,
Buldak is always tangy,
The flavourful taste down your throat,
Seasoned noodles, hot and delicious.

Dhea Mair (12)
Tettenhall College, Tettenhall

Fear

Fear, fear, fear,
Maybe it's everything,
Maybe it's nothing.
Falling, heights,
Maybe even your own reflection.
Maybe fear is taking over,
Maybe it's time to let it go.
Maybe it's time to remove its power,
Maybe it's time to feel empowered,
Maybe fears should be overcome.
Take a stroll, do a roll, find a book you love.
It's all a journey, it all takes time,
So let's raise a beer and face your fears,
Don't let them bring you to tears.

Abigail Davis (12)
Tettenhall College, Tettenhall

The Light That I Am Blind To

When struggles arise and discomfort grows,
When pain, like flora, overgrows,
Temptation that rises and sadness that aches,
Right there, the holy spirit awakes.

You've walked through shadows, bruised and torn,
The enemy will always scorn,
But like a feather to a bird,
You have stuck with me.

So let the world rage all it can,
It has no power against the son of man,
The guilt, the grief, the punishment,
He bore it all.

Jair Benjamin (12)
Tettenhall College, Tettenhall

Grow Wings

One day, I'm gonna grow wings,
So then I can fly in the sky,
So then I can have what I desire.

One day, I'm gonna grow wings,
So then I can stop worrying about the future,
So then I can live right now in the moment.

But how can I grow wings?
Do I have to succeed, die, or get freedom?
Oh dear, I think I repeated 'freedom' too much!

One day, I'm gonna grow wings.

Taisiia Kazakevych (12)
Tettenhall College, Tettenhall

Treading The Boards

The second I step on that stage,
I feel I could stand there for days.
The lights, the glitz, and the high kicks,
Is what makes me feel like a hit.

The backstage buzz,
The mics amped up,
Is truly the best way to feel love,

Never better, never worse,
Just heart and never hurt.

Step on that stage,
And find out where your heart stays.

Amelia Donoghue (15)
Tettenhall College, Tettenhall

Five Seconds From Breaking

For five seconds, can the world stay the same?
For four seconds, can I not feel insane?
For three seconds, can people be kind?
For two seconds, can life be aligned?
For one second, can there be peace?
Just five seconds, side by side, hand in hand,
Accepting we are all unique.

Pennie-May Shaw (16)
Tettenhall College, Tettenhall

My Ginger Hair

This poem's on my hair,
I didn't find it fair.
They'd toy with it, mess with it,
Finally, I'd get over it.
I used to fall, but now I'm tall,
This motto is to never drool,
And fix it.
Now I find it fair,
That I have amazing ginger hair.

Finlay Baldock (12)
Tettenhall College, Tettenhall

Wasps

I do not know why the hive chose me,
Why its warmth felt like something I had missed.
Not love, not quite - but close enough,
To make me ache for every sting I'd bled for.

The attic breathes with golden dread,
A pulse beneath the plaster.
A song too loud, too beautiful,
Too ancient that - I do not know.

And I,
I feel the tremble in my bones,
A rhythm I could not call familiar.
Yet oh, how sweet that buzzing aches,
How the sting unthreads my moan.

There is a wasp's nest in my attic,
A cathedral of wax and war,
Perhaps it sees the cracks in me,
Perhaps it wants me more.

So let them come, those stinging priests,
To soothe this soul they've found,
Let them crawl beneath my ribs,
Let me be taken, I won't ask what for.

Ruan Kellard (15)
The Bishop's Stortford High School, Bishop's Stortford

Pain

Falling down a hole
Darkness surrounds down by the coal
No light, no hope
Yet keep pulling through, trying to cope

Going mad
Possibly a moment had
Passed yet unsure of time
It goes unknown

To all who are around the zone
Noises and sounds making it worse
There it is, that horrible burst
Excruciating

Demobilising
No heat or freezing
Can ever take this away
You become a stray

To yourself
It asserts itself
Over you it looms
From your struggle, it blooms

Yet somehow
One person or maybe more allow
It to ease off for a while
Simply with a smile.

It hurts, yes
But they take away that stress
Panic disappears
Your words not falling on deaf ears.

So never give up and with luck
Find support and hold your head up
And even when your body feels broke
Remember to never give up hope.

Isaac Jones (15)
The Bishop's Stortford High School, Bishop's Stortford

Floundering

Thrashing against the concrete pier
did the waves with perturbed
beat
echo all around.

A solemn union of looming azure and withering grey,
devoid of those hopeful flashes
that make man. Desperate and dismayed.
Perhaps, one could see the beauty in this
struggle
for I cannot. No more. No longer.

A throw or crash with flailing arms
may cry with no call,
a voice unheard in a clamour of silence,
fighting
for a moment's calm, in panic and in pall.

Had he stopped
resisting,
a calmer tide,
with ordered rise and fall,
may meet this land,
in which no thoughts reside,
The Land of the Damned,
a mirror of my lying mind.

Nadim Shawky (15)
The Bishop's Stortford High School, Bishop's Stortford

Empowered

E veryone can reach for the moon
M any reach higher
P eople have great mindsets
O thers work hard for equality, but
W e believe
E veryone can dream a dream that is
R ight or wrong, but
E veryone can believe with the
D epth of their heart

I believe
S chools believe

I n my heart
N o one should be alone

P ower is just a word
E veryone can say it
O nly a few know its true meaning
P eople can be anything they want
L uck is just an adjective
E mbedded in our hearts.

Thomas Cleggett (12)
The Bishop's Stortford High School, Bishop's Stortford

Football

Football, football!
The crowd jeers and cheers
Football, football!
No other feeling like scoring a goal,
Football, football!
The game which goes up and down,
Like a frown...

Football, football!
They all call it a game,
But no, it is a key to the fame.
With twists and turns,
It is such a shame
When people call it a game.

Football is a passion,
For some, it's just a game.
Football.
It's a tough way to climb to the top
Until... chop!
A challenge with too much damage to recover,
Like a lost lover.

Too much passion to carry on.
Football, football...

Luke Thorogood (11)
The Bishop's Stortford High School, Bishop's Stortford

Goals

Always having a goal is great; it inspires you in every way. Once you completed that goal, set a new one, even if you're old.

Stay away from comparison, it's the thief of happiness. Set yourself at a pace a bit higher than comfortable. Having someone who inspires you is great, as long as you don't get jealous to hate.

Always love, there is no room for hate, with that quote there is no debate.

Keeping yourself in a great mindset, I rate.

Without a great mindset you're lost.

Once you've got a mindset, keep it, and show integrity!

Being respectful is only right. Without it you will give people a nasty fright.

Anthony Long (11)
The Bishop's Stortford High School, Bishop's Stortford

Perseverance

P laying with heart, from Highbury to the Emirates,
E very match a battle, every goal resonates,
R ed and white with pride, worn through thick and thin,
S triving for glory, determined to win.
E ven in doubt, they never lose sight,
V ictory is forged through passion and fight.
E ach setback fuels the fire within,
R ising again, where others have been.
A rsenal's legacy, built on belief,
N ever surrender, even through grief.
C hampions in spirit, bold and true,
E ndless resolve - that's what Gunners do.

Ethan Moran (12)

The Bishop's Stortford High School, Bishop's Stortford

Can't You See, Glasses Are Good

Going into my first game of football with my glasses,
Bit nervous of what people think because I want to be a
footballer.
A footballer? people may think!
Yes, a footballer,
But you have glasses?
That's the point I'm trying to prove
I'm just going to make a fool out of you.
You don't see footballers with glasses when playing football.
Some wear contact lenses, but you should be proud to wear
sports glasses.
I want to inspire and make it normal to see people wearing
sports glasses.
People wear them for fashion anyway.
So don't be scared to wear glasses in sport!

Ralf Smith (12)
The Bishop's Stortford High School, Bishop's Stortford

Empowered By Silver

I looked at my rivals,
Judged every face,
But comparison steals joy,
It's not a race.

First match I lost,
Thought he'd be bad,
He beat me fast,
Yeah, that felt sad.

Next one I won,
He was full of pride,
He showed off too much,
I caught him inside.

Third one was lucky,
Not really my plan,
He slipped, I held,
Somehow I ran!

I walked out proud,
With silver in hand,
Stronger than ever,
I now understand.

Codey Taylor-Francis (11)
The Bishop's Stortford High School, Bishop's Stortford

The Night Of The Dambuster

The Lancasters gliding in the air
The Mosquito following behind
The bombs were spinning
Ready to be dropped
The Germans spotted them
The sirens blared

There was panic
Running, screaming below
The bombs were dropped
Bouncing on the water
Destroying the first dam
Panic and screaming
As the water gushed
Two more to go
No need to rush

The next one destroyed
The death below
Can't destroy the last one
Oh well, two will do.

Felix Watson (11)
The Bishop's Stortford High School, Bishop's Stortford

Don't Worry

D o not ever say I can't, as you always can
O ptions are something that not everybody gets, so take them and use them
N ever say never
T here are always two options, so pick the right one

W ho you want to be, is who you're going to be
O kay, be who you want to be
R ight options are the only thing that you know
R eaching for the stars is something you can do
Y ou are great, don't let anybody say you aren't.

Freddie Smith (12)

The Bishop's Stortford High School, Bishop's Stortford

The Greed That Bled The Land

Prominent, mercenary individuals, leading innocents into needless warfare,
They don't just need our good luck prayers,
They need our support:
These people are clueless, they believe the lies, twisted and distorted.

Oh, the cruel hands,
Forming frauds from strands,
Of malice and vengeance,
Yet these leaders feel no penance.

Why just let this happen on?
Whilst they long for brighter days
They will never see,
Due to the corrupt haze.

Finley Morris (12)
The Bishop's Stortford High School, Bishop's Stortford

The Good And Bad Of Life

I feel coldness in the air,
I touch the arrogance of some people,
I hear the disappointment of the spoilt children,
I taste the bitterness of the harsh wind,
I smell the dangerous oil, leaking across the land.
But!
I see the willingness of some people,
I touch the warmness in their hearts,
I hear the enjoyment and thankfulness of children,
I can see the people trying to make a difference!

Xander Spicer (12)
The Bishop's Stortford High School, Bishop's Stortford

Change In The World

The world needs to change
Racism
Sexism
Littering
Bullying
Inequality
The world needs to change
Comparison is the thief of happiness
Disabilities are just abilities
Instead
Be kind
Caring
Loving
Warm-hearted
Thoughtful
And generous
The world needs to change
Everyone needs to help
Change the world.

Jack Wren (11)
The Bishop's Stortford High School, Bishop's Stortford

Be Yourself

B e yourself always,
E ven if it shows how energetic you are,

H ave beliefs about who you want to be,
A lways reach for the stars,
P ersonalities are who you are,
P eople can't change what you are,
Y ou will always be great, and don't let anyone change that.

Dylan McCabe (12)
The Bishop's Stortford High School, Bishop's Stortford

Believe

Everyone needs to believe,
Everyone needs to perceive.
Nobody should be a bully,
We should treat each other fully.

Even in a bad time,
It will soon be fine.
Disability is an ability,
Even if they can't do mobility.

Equality is key,
Even if you do not agree.

Kieran Dedman (12)
The Bishop's Stortford High School, Bishop's Stortford

Equality Is Key

Equality is key
If you want to succeed
Everyone is equal
All you do is believe
Treat people how you would treat yourself
Always have good health
Even if you don't believe
You can succeed
You don't have to be a bully
Treat each other fully
Equality is key.

Oscar Collins (12)
The Bishop's Stortford High School, Bishop's Stortford

Today's A Good Day

Every day, I see a white van
It has a big fan
He says his name is Dan
He has a very big tan

I can see the evergreen trees sway
Tomorrow is my birthday, yay
Today is a good day to be alive
And to thrive
You're always worth it
So go and prove it.

Efe Kakacoglu (12)
The Bishop's Stortford High School, Bishop's Stortford

The Tides Of Change

History, history,
Such a mystery,
Pyramids to skyscrapers,
Swords to atom bombs,
Yet we still have suffering.

Frederick Jobber (13)
The Bishop's Stortford High School, Bishop's Stortford

Power Is Belief

A haiku

Power is belief,
Be positive together,
Believe each other.

Otto Kormis (12)
The Bishop's Stortford High School, Bishop's Stortford

The Screaming Tunnel

You wake up in a deep, dark tunnel,
You light a match,
It goes out as if someone blew it,
You hear an ear-piercing screech,

She's coming,
But not to hurt you,
You feel a presence,
A good one,

It feels like she wants your help to leave,
To face her fears,
You hear a faint voice, "Give me your hand."
"I-I'm scared,"
You hesitate but you hold out your hand

Your hand becomes cold,
She is holding it,
You walk to the end of the tunnel, your hand still cold,
The faint voice returns. "Thank you."

To this day, you're still spooked out,
You decide to research this tunnel,
You find something devastating,
The small girl that you helped,
Had died in that tunnel,

Her house was set on fire,
The reason she is afraid of matches,
That's the cause of her death.

You also find that it was abandoned,
Many, many years ago,
People started vandalising it,
Trying to summon her,

She likes you,
She always has,
You hear a small girl's giggle.

Amy Sutherland (12)
Thornaby Academy, Thornaby

My Little Ballerina

Her feet float across the studio
With a rhythm that no one has ever heard before.
The mirrored walls reflect hundreds of memories,
Each story told in her twirls and leaps.
She dreams of dancing fluidly and elegantly on stage
In front of an audience who have come to see her.
She is my little ballerina!

Under the moonlight's gentle sway,
She pirouettes like a breeze
Brushing through her long velvety hair,
Lost in her hopes and dreams.
She's free in her own world.
She is a determined little girl,
With a gift of her own.
She is my little ballerina!

But behind all of this, she had other feelings.
She hid these feelings from the real world.
She was in pain, but she couldn't help it anymore,
Tears bleeding out of her eyes uncontrollably.
It was hard.
But even with all of these challenges,
She will always be my little ballerina!

Beaux Waterhouse (12)
Thornaby Academy, Thornaby

God's Creation

He will love us enough
His words of grace and compliance
As the consequences of evil gather and grow
The angels will be there to fight with our souls
Although I've never, ever seen them, one thing is true!
They will be there for me when life is tough
And guide me through the dark
May God be with us all
Amen
The presence of God is not a mystery
When we surrender our soul to his will
He sees us as his children of faith
And is willing to forgive and fulfil
He shoulders our troubles and gives us peace.
Flowers, songs, stars, wind, soil, and oceans
We learn that prater is his power of love.
As we struggle to maintain our emotions
We may get lonely but we're never alone
For God knows and feels our woes
He is our lord, saviour, and leader.
He has followed every path we take
He knows we are hesitant and we are tough.

Willow Cooper Wilkinson (11)
Thornaby Academy, Thornaby

Lines Of Power

With pencil poised and paper bare,
A quiet storm begins to flare.
No need for armour, sword, or throne,
In strokes of lead, I stand alone.

A world unfolds beneath my hand,
Where rules are mine to shape and stand.
Each curve, each shade, a whispered roar,
A voice unleashed from the inner core.

When silence lives, now stories speak,
In ink and charcoal bold, not meek.
What once I feared, I now portray,
The shadows chased with light and grey.

I show the strength I didn't see,
The fire I sketch set me free.
Mistakes? They build, they teach, they grow,
Each smudge a part of what I know.

There's power here in every line,
A map of skill by my design.
So when the world feels loud and vast,
I draw a breath and draw it fast.
For in these lines I rise, I stand,
A universe held in my hand.

Michelle Fegbada (13)
Thornaby Academy, Thornaby

Chasing Shadows Through The Lyrics

In the digital realms where rhythms play,
Alex Warren crafts his vivid array.
With melodies woven from heart and soul,
So out of the ordinary, making troubled waters whole.

Through gentle strums and soaring notes,
He paints the silence, as emotion floats.
With lyrics that echo the dance of the night,
Each song carries you home, giving light.

From whispers of longing to shouts of delight,
His voice captures moments, both tender and bright.
Burning Down, a story unfolds,
Of dreams and adventures, both daring and bold.

With fans in the crowd, a united embrace,
In harmony, they find their place.
So let the sound waves change your mind,
With Alex Warren's music, you'll find who you are.

I'll save you a seat,
You'll be alright, kid.
As the Yard Sale begins,
Remember me happy.

Lillie Manning (15)
Thornaby Academy, Thornaby

The Battlefield

S o while you think that the battle wasn't great, think again because it was at an extremely high rate.

P eople fought, people brought, but little did they know, this battle would lead them to their fate.

I t was quite worrying, especially because of what was at stake, but our armies and Spitfires made other countries quake.

T remble they did, tried to get rid, a bigger challenge indeed. And awful waste of a quid.

F rom oceans to regions, to countries worldwide, the British had caused a colossal tide.

I n dominance, power, and intelligence, the Brits had the upper hand, whereas other countries couldn't stand.

R eady and prepared, the British had fought. Unfortunately, some were shot. They had lost the lot.

E xtraordinary, that's why we celebrate the 8th of May, with a special day called VE Day.

Ralphy Dollard (12)
Thornaby Academy, Thornaby

My Body

You are not the victim
You are a puppet
Brainwashed by society's views on your own body shape
Struggling to escape
Fighting the urge to not look at the calories
Somebody get me out of here please
Suddenly, I can finally eat normally
But the next day the food on my plate glares at me abnormally
Staring loathfully at my rival in the mirror
The feral and fractus whispers getting nearer
Exercising till my body feels numb
What kind of person have I become?
Gradually, what I see before the mirror doesn't cause me stress
I love the tranquillity I can now access
Participating in activities only for my health
I love this new kind of wealth
Knowing that many girls like me now feel confident
Although our struggle needs some acknowledgement
Stop being the puppet
Be the puppeteer.

Mirab Shahzad (14)
Thornaby Academy, Thornaby

The Truth Of Covid-19

C ase numbers rise every day, is this virus here to stay?

O ur world is fighting this dreadful disease, bringing Britain to its knees.

R ules must be obeyed, stay home, stay safe, and don't be afraid.

O n my birthday, I had to celebrate alone, at least I had my iPhone.

N ew year, new start as lockdown keeps us all apart.

"A rise, Sir Tom," said the Queen with social distancing in between.

V irus leaves you short of breath, don't let this be your early death.

I solate, vaccinate, and find new ways to communicate.

R etired nurses go back to work, all they see is pain and hurt.

U ncool people won't follow rules, so this means I have to be homeschooled.

S o please stay home, stay safe, and let's not meet at Heaven's gate.

Harley Alyssa-May Atkins (12)

Thornaby Academy, Thornaby

Don't Be Afraid To Be Unique

Feelings are important to me,
being fine isn't something I know how to be.
No one knows about the tears on my face,
no one sees that I process things at my own pace.
I have a heart of sorrow,
remind myself to make it to tomorrow.
Even if every day I feel low,
I manage to survive every episode.
A face full of smiles I wear,
pain deep inside but I grin and I bear.
I sit still with a fixed but broken glare,
even through misery, I show that I care.
Emotions are things I'm passionate about,
we should be heard,
we should not have to shout,
so please don't be afraid to speak,
don't be afraid to be unique,
there are always people who are there to support you,
always people who will help when you're blue.

Autumn Day (13)

Thornaby Academy, Thornaby

Nature's Neglect

Deep in the woods where animals rest,
The birds lay down in their snug nests.
People come to cut down trees,
The fishes watch sadly from the now dull streams.

The owl's home is taken away,
More and more are taken every day.
The many animals now have no homes,
The logs get covered in the sea's foam.

All day and night they build and build,
They hammer and hammer, drill and drill.
Once it's done, they finally settle,
Happy their home is as strong as metal.

Finally, there's peace at last,
All the animals are having a blast.
Everything goes back to normal life.
Even the farmer and his nervous wife.

Sophie Iveson (11)
Thornaby Academy, Thornaby

The Silence Of War

In fields once ripe with laughter's cheer,
Now echoes whisper, haunting near.
The broken ground, a solemn stage,
Where dreams lie still, and hopes disengage.

A silence pulls, so thick, so deep,
Where vibrant souls no longer weep.
The drums of battle cease their sound,
In ghostly shadows, peace is found.

Forgotten are the soldiers' cries,
The valorous hopes, the battle lies.
In whispered thoughts and silent prayers,
We mourn the loss and the weight it bears.

Yet in this silence a promise glows,
Of healing hearts and softer touches.
For when the silence covers the land,
A quiet strength begins to stand.

Reece Taylor (14)
Thornaby Academy, Thornaby

Football Players

They call our field iron
They call our ball a pigskin
They call our players athletes
But I don't know where to begin
All football players are athletes
But not all athletes play this game
We make more than a contract
Collision sports is a better name.
We process an inner toughness
An iron will that eases pain
Those who don't play football
May think that we're deranged
We hit, we run, we punt, we pass
We play in mud or on the grass
I hope this game will make us men
That we show courage when we lose
And grace when we win
I really hope to be a footballer one day.

Kacey-May Lenighan (12)
Thornaby Academy, Thornaby

Fair And Square Truth

In the halls where silence holds breath,
Where truth must rise or fall to death,
There walks a force both firm and fair,
Justice with an unyielding stare.

Though shadows stretch and show rage,
She writes her name in every page,
Where courage speaks and wrongs are righted,
Where broken lives are proven right.

Justice stands with even hand,
Not swayed by power, wealth, or land,
She sees through masks like thin disguise
She walks with purpose, not a dream.

In silent courts and open skies,
Justice lives where truth still lies.

Kejsi Diva (12)
Thornaby Academy, Thornaby

Words Of Empowerment

When I pick up that pen, I feel empowered,
Like words on the page are getting louder and louder.
And the words are coming to your mind with such power.
When I write, I feel a subtle spark,
Like a fire caught within the dark.
With each verse I speak my mind,
Not afraid of what people may find.
From a whisper to a loud voice,
I always find my choice.
It's not within the sword or throne,
It's the lives I changed with words I wrote.
From my heart to my soul I will not be tamed,
Because in every poem I write, I am exclaimed.

Rutaab Asim (13)
Thornaby Academy, Thornaby

In My Dreams

Within the quiet corners of my mind
A sanctuary where I often find
A refuge built from whispered dreams
A space where silent hope softly gleams
My self-place, a gentle, sacred land
Where I can breathe just as I am
A harbour of endless hues
Where whispers of the night become morning's muse
Soft shadows dance upon the silver stream
Carrying the night's embrace
I soar through realms unseen
Forevermore, in dreams, the soul is free to trace
The boundless depths of time and space.

Patience Micah (14)
Thornaby Academy, Thornaby

Justice

Murder is wrong
And we should all know it
But where is the justice for those who were killed?
Now that's just barbaric

To the innocent who got murdered
By just existing
Now that's just absurd

Murder is ugly, scary and cruel
Now justice should be served
To the families of the victims
They should be put in prison
For the rest of their lives
To think about the pain and suffering
They have caused
Justice is served!

Felicity Robson (12)
Thornaby Academy, Thornaby

The Silent Dance Of Books

In realms of paper, bound in ink,
My heart finds solace, I truly think.
Each page a journey, a world to see,
Books, oh books, how I love thee.

Through tales of old and stories new,
I lose myself, my spirit renew.
With every chapter, a bond so deep,
In the world of books, my secrets I keep.

So let me wander, forever roam,
In libraries vast, my happy home.
For in the pages, my soul takes flight,
Books, my passion, my guiding light.

Scarlett Foster (12)
Thornaby Academy, Thornaby

A Spark Of Hope

In shadows deep, where worries reside,
A tiny spark, where hope does hide.
A gentle whisper in the breeze,
Rustling softly through the trees.

A fragile seed in barren land,
Reaching for light with steady hand.
A promise whispered, soft and low,
Of brighter days and skies aglow.

Though storms may rage and darkness loom,
Hope's ember glows within the gloom.
A beacon bright, a guiding star,
Leading us forward, near and far.

Amelia Galloway (11)
Thornaby Academy, Thornaby

Dragons

D ragons thought to be just a myth 'til a red one showed itself.

R oaming after the domination of the human race we used to know.

A rmies wiped even with the guns and weaponry they had.

G inormous creatures controlling the land we used to reign.

O nto a new era, the globe experiences.

N ew beginnings open up as their legacy continues.

S urvivors and supplies dwindling in numbers...

Tyler Hobbs (12)

Thornaby Academy, Thornaby

We Can Make A Change!

Pollution is happening every minute
Which brings us down
Deforestation is giving us nothing
But leads to death
We need to save our environment
Because humans can end up extinct as well
Hoping one day we don't litter
Is like a dream
That wouldn't happen if I tried
But if we try and keep our Earth hygienic
We can make change
Can we?

Sienna Trotter (11)
Thornaby Academy, Thornaby

Princess Bella

Princess Bella, what is she?
She's fluffy, adorable, and
As cute as can be.

She can sleep the clock around,
She hides in places she can't be found.

Playing with her toys on grass so green,
Among the trees she can be seen.

She likes to go out in mist and fog,
What is she?
She is my dog!

Sophie Wendy Bown (12)
Thornaby Academy, Thornaby

Beauty Through Different Eyes

Beauty, a rare weapon,
Which can create war and love
Something that can differ from one perspective to another
Found in everything.
But have you seen it?
It's all about how you see it
It's something that impacts your decisions.
Beauty -
Not only pleases our eyes
But hits our hearts hard.

Sreya Sujith Nair (14)
Thornaby Academy, Thornaby

Eating Flowers

I'm sitting in the garden
Eating lots of flowers
I can sit and eat them all
For hours and hours

Dandelions are my favourite
So pretty, fluffy flowers
I can walk and pick them all
For hours and hours.

Nellie Henry (12)
Thornaby Academy, Thornaby

Vampire In The Woods

It was a dark night
I was all alone
My vampire's transformation kicked in
I could smell human blood
I was hungry for it
I ran for it at nearly 200mph
My big fangs went into the side of their throat
Sucking all the blood out of their body
I never knew the friend was with them
It jumped my mind - another human
I sucked all the blood out of their body
I was thirsty for human blood
I could smell it even from a thousand miles away
I was bloodthirsty
I went on a bloodlust rampage
I killed eight people
A few hours went by
I killed eight more
A few hours went past
And I knew I had to get out of my vampire form.

Cian Dooley (11)
Venture Academy, Henley-In-Arden

The Lovely Layla

L ovely, kind
A nd caring
Y ou always make me giggle
L aughing
A ll the time, you are

S o special to me
H elping me
E very day
P eople love
H aving you around
E veryone thinks you are
R elaxed and
D etermined to do things to help everyone.

Chloe Roebuck (16)

Venture Academy, Henley-In-Arden

The Beauty Of Nature

Visual beauty under the sun
Makes people have a lot of fun.

The wind blows gently by the sea
The breeze is free
To all people of any nationality.

Everyone has a lot of fun
Down by the beach, under the sun.

Quinn Vickery (13)
Venture Academy, Henley-In-Arden

Earth

E   ggs are frying in a pan
A   nimals are hunting for food
R   ecycle to make new things
T   rees are homes for creatures
H   umans must stop deforestation.

George Derry (12)
Venture Academy, Henley-In-Arden

The End Of The World

Upon us reigns the fear of death
With them and all
We run and hide
From the war of the worlds.

Josh Edwards (16)
Venture Academy, Henley-In-Arden